9-1 GCSE NOTES GEORGE ORWELL'S *ANIMAL FARM* - Study guide (All chapters, page-by-page analysis)

by Joe Broadfoot

All rights reserved

Copyright © Joe Broadfoot, 2016

The right of Joe Broadfoot to be identified as the author of this work has been asserted in accordance with Section 77 of the Copyright, Designs and Patents Act 1988

ISBN-13:
978-1537450995

ISBN-10:
1537450999

9-1 GCSE REVISION NOTES – ANIMAL FARM

CONTENTS

Introduction 3
Best Essay Practice 4
Essay planning 5
New specification 8
Chapter One 14
Chapter Two 18
Chapter Three 22
Chapter Four 25
Chapter Five 28
Chapter Six 31
Chapter Seven 35
Chapter Eight 39
Chapter Nine 44
Chapter Ten 48
Essay Writing Tips 52
Glossary 57

9-1 GCSE REVISION NOTES – ANIMAL FARM

Best essay practice

There are so many way to write an essay. Many schools use **PEE** for paragraphs: point/evidence/explain. Others use **PETER**: point/evidence/technique/explain/reader; **PEEL**: point, example, explain, link; **PEEE**: point/evidence/explain/explore. Whichever method you use, make sure you mention the **writer's effects**. This generally is what most students forget to add. You must think of what the writer is trying to achieve by using a particular technique and what is actually achieved. Do not just spot techniques and note them. You may get some credit for using appropriate technology, but unless you can comment on the effect created on the reader and/or the writer's intention, you will miss out on most of the marks available.

Brief Introduction

This book is aimed at GCSE students of English Literature who are studying George Orwell's *Animal Farm*. The focus is on what examiners are looking for, especially since the changes to the curriculum in 2015, and here you will find each chapter covered in detail. I hope this will help you and be a valuable tool in your studies and revision.

Criteria for high marks

Make sure you use appropriate critical language (see glossary of literary terms at the back). You need your argument to be fluent, well-structured and coherent. Stay focused!

Analyse and explore the use of form, structure and the language. Explore how these aspects affect the meaning.

Make connections between texts and look at different interpretations. Explore their strengths and weaknesse Don't forget to use supporting references to strength argument.

Analyse and explore the context.

Essay planning

In order to write a good essay it is necessary to plan. In fact, it is best to quite formulaic in an exam situation, as you won't have much time to get started. Therefore I will ask you to learn the following acronym: **DATMC (Definition, Application, Terminology, Main, Conclusion**. Some schools call it: **GSLMC (General, Specific, Link, Main, Conclusion)**, but it amounts to the same thing. The first three letters concern the introduction. (Of course, the alternative is to leave some blank lines and write your introduction after you have completed the main body of your essay, but it is probably not advisable for most students).

Let us first look at the following exam question, which is on poetry (of course, the same essay-planning principles apply to essays on novels and plays as well).

QUESTION: Explore how the poet conveys **feelings** in the poem.

STEP ONE: Identify the **keyword** in the question. (I have already done this, by highlighting it in **bold**). If you are following GSLMC, you now need to make a **general statement** about what feelings are. Alternatively, if you're following DATMC, simply **define** 'feelings'. For example, 'Feelings are emotion states or reactions or vague, irrationals ideas and beliefs'.

9-1 GCSE REVISION NOTES – ANIMAL FARM

STEP TWO: If you are following GSLMC, you now need to make a **specific statement** linking feelings (or whatever else you've defined) to how they appear in the poem. Alternatively, if you're following DATMC, simply define which 'feelings' **apply** in this poem. For example, 'The feelings love, fear and guilt appear in this poem, and are expressed by the speaker in varying degrees.'

STEP THREE: If you are following GSLMC, you now need to make a **link statement** identifying the methods used to convey the feelings (or whatever else you've defined) in the poem. Alternatively, if you're following DATMC, simply define which **techniques** are used to convey 'feelings' in this poem. For example, 'The poet primarily uses alliteration to emphasise his heightened emotional state, while hyperbole and enjambment also help to convey the sense that the speaker is descending into a state of madness.

STEP FOUR: Whether you are following GSLMC or DATMC, the next stage is more or less the same. The main part of the essay involves writing around **six paragraphs**, using whichever variation of PEEE you prefer. In my example, I will use **Point, Evidence, Exploration, Effect** on the listener. To make your essay even stronger, try to use your quotations chronologically. It will be easier for the examiner to follow, which means you are more likely to achieve a higher grade. To be more specific, I recommend that you take and analyse two quotations from the beginning of the poem, two from the middle, and two at the end.

STEP FIVE: Using Carol Ann Duffy's poem, 'Stealing', here's an example of how you could word one of your six paragraphs: **(POINT)** 'Near the beginning of the poem, the speaker's determination is expressed.' **(EVIDENCE)** 'This is achieved through the words: 'Better off dead than giving in'. **(EXPLORATION).** The use of 'dead' emphasizes how far the speaker is prepared to go in pursuit of what he wants, although there is a sense that he is exaggerating (hyperbole). **(EFFECT)** The listener senses that the speaker may be immature given how prone he is to exaggerate his own bravery.

STEP SIX: After writing five or more paragraphs like the one above, it will be time to write a **conclusion**. In order to do that, it is necessary to sum up your previous points and evaluate them. This is not the time to introduce additional quotations. Here is an example of what I mean: 'To conclude, the poet clearly conveys the speaker's anger. Although the listener will be reluctant to completely sympathise with a thief, there is a sense that the speaker is suffering mentally, which makes him an interesting and partially a sympathetic character. By using a dramatic monologue form, the poet effectively conveys the speaker's mental anguish, which makes it easier to more deeply understand what first appears to be inexplicable acts of violence.

Other tips

Make your studies active!

9-1 GCSE REVISION NOTES – ANIMAL FARM

Don't just sit there reading! Never forget to annotate, annotate and annotate!

Other tips

Make your studies active!

Don't just sit there reading! Never forget to annotate, annotate and annotate!

All page references refer to the 2000 reprinted paperback edition of *Animal Farm* published by Penguin Classics, London (ISBN: 978-0-141-18270-4).

Animal Farm

AQA (New specification starting in 2015)

If you're studying for an AQA qualification in English Literature, there's a good chance your teachers will choose this text to study. There are good reasons for that: it's moralistic in that the text encourages us to think about right and wrong.

Animal Farm is one of the texts listed on Paper 2, which needs to be completed in 2 hours 15 minutes. Your writing on the essay will only be part of the exam, however, and for the rest of time you will need to write about poetry: two poems categorised as 'Unseen Poetry' and two poems from the AQA anthology.

AQA have given students a choice of 12 set texts for the Modern Texts section of the exam paper. There are 6 plays: JB Priestley's *An Inspector Calls*, Willy Russell's *Blood Brothers*, Alan Bennett's *The History Boys*, Dennis Kelly's *DNA*, Simon Stephens's script of *The Curious Incident of the Dog in the Night-Time*, and Shelagh Delaney's *A Taste of Honey*. Alternatively, students can chose to write on the following 6 novels: William Golding's *Lord of the Flies*, AQA's Anthology called *Telling Tales*, George Orwell's *Animal Farm*, Kazuo Ishiguro's *Never Let Me Go*, Meera Syal's *Anita and Me*, and Stephen Kelman's *Pigeon English*. Answering one essay question on one of the above is worth a total of 34 marks, which includes 4 for vocabulary, spelling, punctuation and grammar. In other words, this section is worth 21.25% of your total grade at GCSE.

AQA have produced a poetry anthology entitled *Poems, Past and Present*, which includes 30 poems. Rather than study all 30, students are to study one of the two clusters of 15, which concentrate on common themes. There are two themes which students can choose from: Love and relationships, or power and conflict. Within the chosen thematic cluster, students must study all 15 poems and be prepared to write on any of them. Answering this section is worth 18.75% of your total GCSE grade.

The 'unseen poetry' section is more demanding, in that students will not know what to expect. However, as long as they are prepared to comment and compare different poems in terms of their content, theme, structure and language, students should be ready for

9-1 GCSE REVISION NOTES – ANIMAL FARM

whatever the exam can throw at them. This section is worth 20% of your total grade at GCSE.

Paper 2 itself makes up 60% of your total grade or, in other words, 96 raw marks. Just under half of those marks, 44 to be exact (27.5% of 60%), can be gained from analysing how the writer uses language, form and structure to create effects. To get a high grade, it is necessary for students to use appropriate literary terms, like metaphors, similes and so on.

AO1 accounts for 36 marks of the total of 96 (22.5% of the 60% for Paper 2, to be exact). To score highly on AO1, students need to provide an informed personal response, using quotations to support their point of view.

AO3 is all about context and, like Paper 1, only 7.5% of the total mark is awarded for this knowledge (12 marks). Similarly, AO4 (which is about spelling, punctuation and grammar) only accounts for 2.5% of the total (4 marks).

One of the difficulties with Paper 1 is the language. That can't be helped, bearing in mind that part A of the exam paper involves answering questions on Shakespeare, whereas part B is all about the 19th-century novel.

To further complicate things, the education system is in a state of flux: that means we have to be ready for constant change. Of course, everyone had got used to grades A,B and C meaning a pass. It was simple, it was straightforward and nearly everyone understood it. Please be prepared that from this day henceforward, the top grade will now be known as 9. A grade 4 will be a pass, and anything below that will be found and anything above it will be a pass. Hopefully, that's not too confusing for anyone!

Now onto the exam itself. As I said, Paper 1 consists of Shakespeare and the 19th-century novel. Like Paper 2, it is a written closed book exam (in other words you are not allowed to have the texts with you), which lasts one hour 45 minutes. You can score 64 marks, which amounts to 40% of your GCSE grade.

In section B, students will be expected to write in detail about an extract from the novel they have studied in class and then write about the novel as a whole. Just for the record, the choices of novel are the following: *The Strange Case of Dr Jekyll and Mr Hyde* by Robert Louis Stevenson, *A Christmas Carol* and *Great Expectations* by Charles Dickens, *Jane Eyre* by Charlotte Brontë, *Frankenstein* by Mary Shelley, *Pride and Prejudice* by Jane Austin, and *The Sign of Four* by Sir Arthur Conan Doyle.

Another important thing to consider is the fact that for section B of Paper 1, you will not be assessed on Assessment Objective 4 (AO4), which involves spelling, punctuation, grammar and vocabulary. This will be assessed on section A of Paper 1, which is about Shakespeare, and it will be worth 2.5% of your overall GCSE grade. In terms of raw marks, it is worth 4 out of

9-1 GCSE REVISION NOTES – ANIMAL FARM

64. So for once, we need not concern ourselves with what is affectionately known as 'SPAG' too much on this part of Paper 1.

However, it is necessary to use the correct literary terminology wherever possible to make sure we maximise our marks on Assessment Objective2 (AO2). AO2 tests how well we can analyse language form and structure. Additionally, we are expected to state the effect the writer tried to create and how it impacts on the reader.

This brings me onto Assessment Objective 1 (AO1), which involves you writing a personal response to the text. It is important that you use quotations to backup your points of view. Like AO2, AO1 is worth 15% of your GCSE on Paper 1.

Assessment Objective 3 (AO3) is worth half of that, but nevertheless it is important to comment on context to make sure you get as much of the 7.5% up for grabs as you can.

So just to make myself clear, there are 30 marks available in section B for your answer on the 19th-century novel. Breaking it down even further, you will get 12 marks maximum the backing up your personal opinion with quotations, an additional 12 marks for analysing the writer's choice of words for effect (not forgetting to use appropriate terminology - more on that see the glossary at the back of this book), and six marks for discussing context.

As you can see, we've got a lot to get through so without further ado let's get on with the actual text itself and possible exam questions.

Previous exam questions

Notwithstanding the governmental changes to the grading system, it is still good practice to go over previous exam papers. To make sure that you meet AQA's learning objectives and get a high mark, make sure you go into the exam knowing something about the following:

- the plot
- the characters
- the theme
- selected quotations/details
- exam skills

9-1 GCSE REVISION NOTES – ANIMAL FARM

Page-by-page analysis

Chapter One

The chapter begins with a portrayal of the owner of Manor Farm, Mr Jones. We don't find out his first name, and this depersonalises him, making him less sympathetic as a character. We discover he is 'too drunk' to be really good at his job (1). The farmer's wife seems almost pig-like, as she is portrayed 'snoring', which makes a sound similar to a pig's snort (1).

The next character we are introduced to is a 'prize Middle White boar' called 'Old Major' (1). His exhibition name is 'Willingdon Beauty', which feminises him somewhat (1). Nevertheless, he is 'highly regarded' by the animals, even if the human beings see him as something of a trophy (1).

Old Major exudes power. That's clear from his portrayal as 'a majestic-looking pig' (1, 2). The word 'majestic' is often associated with royalty, making him sound like a natural leader.

The other animals have gathered to hear him speak and they include 'the two cart-horses, Boxer and Clover' (2). Despite their 'vast hairy hoofs', they take 'great care' not to trample on the smaller animals (2). From the outset, these two characters are portrayed as warm and kind.

Benjamin is another significant character, who receives some attention from the narrator. He seems to be genuinely 'devoted to Boxer' and although the pair graze side by side on Sundays 'never speaking', there seems to be something decent and honest about their relationship (2). The fact that they are together on the holiest day of the week shows there is something pure about their friendship, despite Benjamin's tendency to be 'cynical' (2).

Juxtaposed with Benjamin is Mollie, 'the foolish, pretty white mare' (3). She is portrayed 'mincing daintily in, chewing at a lump of sugar' (3). She seems extremely superficial, wanting everything to be sugar-coated like sugar. She is mostly concerned with her appearance and her 'red ribbons' (3).

Old Major launches into his speech when most of the animals are assembled, using emotive language to motivate them into realising their piteous state. For instance, he says: 'We are slaughtered with hideous cruelty' (4). The

9-1 GCSE REVISION NOTES – ANIMAL FARM

personal pronoun 'we' includes all the animals and makes them feel more affected. Additionally, 'slaughtered' sounds more emotive than 'killed', so the effect of it is to enrage the animals (4) The same goes for 'hideous' and 'cruelty' (4).

The old pig manipulates the animals with his clever use of language, asking rhetorical questions like: 'And you hens, how many eggs have you laid [...]?' (5). Clearly, the hens are unlikely to remember the exact number, but they will know that none or few 'hatched into chickens', which emphasises Old Major's point that the animals are being oppressed (5).

As he nears the end of his speech, the animals take a vote on whether or not 'wild creatures, such as rats and rabbits' are 'friends' or 'enemies' (6). We find out that the cat is particularly untrustworthy, as it 'was discovered to have voted on both sides (6).

Old Major warns the animals not to become like Man. He sets down a number of rules, which are phrased negatively: 'No animal must ever live in a house, or sleep in a bed, or wear clothes, or drink alcohol, or smoke tobacco, or touch money, or engage in trade' (7).

The old pig begins to teach the other animals a forgotten song, entitled 'Beasts of England' (7). Most striking arguably is the personification of the 'cruel whips' which 'no more shall crack' (8). The innate cruelty of using the whips is emphasised by the use of the literary device.

We soon realise which animals are the most intelligent, based on their ability to learn the song. The narrator tells us: 'The clever ones, such as the pigs and dogs, they had the whole song by heart within a few minutes' (9).

9-1 GCSE REVISION NOTES – ANIMAL FARM

Chapter Two

The old Major, who has been compared to Russian revolutionary leader Vladimir Lenon by many critics, dies 'peacefully in his sleep' after delivering his speech (10).

Thereafter, we meet 'two young boars named Snowball and Napoleon' (10). The latter is described as a 'large, rather fierce-looking Berkshire boar'. He sounds quite formidable, but distinguished by virtue of being 'the only Berkshire on the farm' (10). Like Benjamin, he's 'not much of a talker', but unlike the aforementioned donkey, Napoleon does not have any sympathetic qualities. Even his name reminds us of France's all-conquering emperor of the eighteen and nineteenth century, who was almost unbeatable on the battlefield.

Meanwhile, Snowball is more 'vivacious' or lively. Additionally, he is 'more inventive', so seems to be the more original thinker of the two (10). The name suggests purity of thought like unadulterated snow. However, he and his idea may be discarded or thrown away as easily as a snowball.

A third pig is mentioned: Squealer. He is described as having 'very round cheeks, twinkling eyes, nimble movements and a shrill voice' (10). We are warned that he is 'somehow very persuasive' (11). His name suggests that he is like an empty vessel making the most the noise. Much of that noise is unpleasantly shrill because of his voice, but we suspect the content of what he says may be just as unpalatable.

We hear that Mollie's questions run contrary to the spirit of Animalism, 'old Major's teachings' condensed 'into a complete system of thought (11). She concerns herself with 'sugar' and 'ribbons', the trappings of the old regime (11).

Aside from Mollie's materialist and counter-revolutionary aspirations, the Rebellion has to deal with ideas put about by 'Moses, the tame raven' (12). He talks of 'Sugarcandy Mountain, to which all animals' go when they die (12). Despite the grandness of the promises of 'Sunday seven days a week', 'some of them believed in Sugarcandy Mountain' (12). This shows how gullible the animals are. Of course, Moses is supposed to represent a religious figure. Like a vicar wearing predominantly black, Moses's feathers are the same colour. Additionally, the name Moses is Biblical, so

9-1 GCSE REVISION NOTES – ANIMAL FARM

there is no doubt the raven is religious in this allegory.

The revolution arrives spontaneously, as 'nothing of the kind had been planned beforehand' (13). Mr Jones and his men live to rue not 'bothering to feed the animals' as it results in their 'sudden uprising' (13).

After the overthrow of the humans, the animals are initially surprised. The writer uses emotive language to describe objects associated with Mr Jones's reign: 'cruel knives' and 'degrading nosebags' (14).

Nevertheless, the animals still respect their former master, judging by their behaviour when they enter the farmhouse. They whisper and gaze 'with a kind of awe' (15).

Only Mollie seems to disagree with the consensus. She is caught with 'a piece of blue ribbon [...] admiring herself in the glass in a very foolish manner' (16). She is vain and cares little for the revolution or their principles.

Although 'the seven commandments' are emblazoned on the wall, the spelling mistake of 'friend' does not augur well for the animals' future (17). It seems they can expect to be treated fiendishly rather than in a friendly manner.

Soon afterwards, Napoleon shows a propensity to deceive the other animals, telling them the milk 'will be attended to' (18). When they return in the evening, the milk has mysteriously 'disappeared' (18).

9-1 GCSE REVISION NOTES – ANIMAL FARM

Chapter Three

Although we hear 'the harvest was an even bigger success than' the animals had hoped for, the fact that the pigs do 'not actually work' sounds ominous (19). Their direction and supervision may be welcome, but surely they could lend a hand as well, if all animals are truly equal.

Using alliteration, the writer emphasizes the delicious taste of the animals' own produce: 'Every mouthful was an acute positive pleasure' (20).

Similarly, alliteration makes us fully realize how hard Boxer works. The plosive sounds of the 'p's in 'pushing and pulling' reminds us of the physical effort involved in farming, especially for such a committed worker whose motto is: 'I will work harder' (20).

Meanwhile, Boxer's friend, Benjamin, is an opposite when it comes to work ethic, 'never volunteering for extra work' (21). He is 'quite unchanged since the Rebellion', continuing to be 'obstinate' and 'cryptic' (21). The donkey is not as easily influenced as Boxer and the other animals.

We discover that Snowball and Napoleon 'were never in agreement' (22). This seems to indicate that there will be a rift between them in the future.

Snowball appears to be industrious as he is 'indefatigable' when it comes to 'organizing the other animals into what he called Animal Committees' (22). However, aside from 'reading and writing' classes, a lot of his grand projects end in 'failure' (22).

The narrator then tells us which animals are the best readers. We can infer that dogs are intelligent, but chose to concentrate on 'the Seven Commandments' (23). This shows us that they are only interested in commands; they don't want to think for themselves.

Snowball condenses the commandments down to a simple maxim: 'FOUR LEGS GOOD, TWO LEGS BAD' (24). The sheep develop 'a great liking for this maxim', bleating it in unison. Snowball is working incredibly hard to make Animalism accessible to all, while Napoleon takes no interest in Snowball's projects.

9-1 GCSE REVISION NOTES – ANIMAL FARM

However, Napoleon does show an interest in Jessie and Bluebell's 'nine study puppies' (25). He takes them 'up into a loft', making 'himself responsible for their education' (25). It sounds ominous, as we don't know exactly what Napoleon is up to, at this stage.

Meanwhile, Squealer has emerged as the spokesman for the pigs, explaining that apples and milk have to be consumed by them, 'the brainworkers' (25). It's just 'to preserve' their 'health' (25). He manipulates the other animals by preying on their fears of their old master returning as 'if there was one thing that the animals were completely certain of, it was that they did not want Jones back' (26)

Chapter Four

A propaganda war has been started, with Snowball and Napoleon sending out 'flights of pigeons' for that purpose (27). Their specific instructions are to 'mingle with the animals on neighbouring farms, tell them the story of the Rebellion, and teach them the tune of "Beasts of England"' (27). As this is an allegorical novel, historical parallels can be found in the Russians' attempt to spread the word of communism throughout the world.

Meanwhile, we find out that Mr Jones has not changed: he is still drinking to excess. He looks to other farmers frequenting 'the Red Lion at Willingdon' for sympathy, but no help is offered at first (27).

We get the impression that all the farmers are corrupt, as 'at heart, each of them' secretly wonders how to 'turn Jones's misfortune to his own advantage' (27). Their behaviour could be said to resemble politicians, particularly in the field of foreign policy, where alliances are quickly drawn and shelved whenever convenient.

9-1 GCSE REVISION NOTES – ANIMAL FARM

Two farmers eventually take an interest: Mr Pilkington, an 'easy-going gentleman-farmer' who owns Foxwood and, Mr Frederick, 'a tough, shrewd man, perpetually involved in lawsuits and with a name for driving hard bargains' (27, 28). The latter is such a penny-pincher that it's no wonder that his farm is called 'Pinchfield' (27).

Through personification, the writer emphasises how powerful the message coming from Animal Farm is. Even the song is 'irrepressible' (28). It seems as if the song has a life of its own and it cannot be killed.

Similarly, personification emphasises the danger of the gun fired at Snowball in 'The Battle of The Cowshed'. When we hear how 'the pellets scored bloody streaks along Snowball's back', we acknowledge how the pellets move, scratching grooves into the pig's flesh. Like the song, the pellets seem alive and dangerous.

Nevertheless, the animals are victorious. Boxer, in particular, is mortified at the cost of victory, 'pawing with his hoof at the stable-lad who lay face down in the mud' (31). He speaks 'sorrowfully', but is reprimanded by Snowball for showing 'sentimentality' (31). For the reader, Boxer's remorse makes him a more sympathetic character than Snowball, who states: 'The only good human being is a dead one' (31).

Mollie, meanwhile, is 'found hiding in a stall with her head buried among the hay in the manger. This is ostrich-like, head-in-the-sand behaviour makes her unsympathetic in comparison to the valiant Boxer. The contrast with his selflessness makes her seem all the more selfish.

Although the ambush was planned, the narrator suggests that the victory 'celebration' is 'impromptu' (32). However, so much is planned in Animal Farm, it seems unlikely that any official celebration would be improvised; therefore, the word 'impromptu' may be ironic.

9-1 GCSE REVISION NOTES – ANIMAL FARM

Chapter Five

The focus is on Mollie here, with her being portrayed 'foolishly gazing at her own reflection in the water' (33). Clover confronts her about fraternising with 'one of Mr Pilkington's men' and although Mollie denies it, her guilt is confirmed by the discovery of 'a little pile of lump sugar and several bunches of ribbon' (34). Unsurprisingly, Mollie disappears and is next seen pulling 'a smart dogcart' for 'a red-faced man [...] who looked like a publican'. It seems that she preferred Animal Farm when it was owned by a drunken Mr Jones, for she has chosen a master who also appears to be fond of alcohol.

With Mollie becoming a taboo subject after her departure, the focus shifts to the unforgiving January weather and the arguments between Snowball and Napoleon. When it comes to garnering support, the latter is 'especially successfully with the sheep' (35).

Meanwhile, Snowball's approach is more intellectual, a bit like Trostky's when he was up against Stalin after Lenin's death. Snowball talks 'learnedly' and the animals listen 'in astonishment' (35). His plans for the windmill become so 'complicated' that the other animals find them 'completely unintelligible' (36).

Napoleon shows his utter contempt for Snowball when we hear that he 'urinated over the plans and walked out' (36). Needless to say, this does not bode well for Snowball.

The two leaders seem to be constantly at loggerheads, and each creates his own slogan: 'Vote for Snowball and the three-day week' and 'Vote for Napoleon and the full manger' (37). Of the two, Snowball seems more peaceful, as he advocates sending 'out more and more pigeons' to 'stir up rebellion' elsewhere (37). By contrast, Napoleon believes they must 'procure firearms and train themselves in the use of them' (37). It seems that with such diametrically opposed views, conflict is inevitable.

Although Snowball's argument is stronger, Napoleon utters 'a high-pitched whimper' to summon his 'nine enormous dogs wearing brass-studded collars' to settle the dispute (38, 39). Snowball is chased away and escapes through 'a hole in the hedge' (39).

With his rival gone, Napoleon begins to enforce his will. We discover there will be 'no more debates' (40). No one can argue, thanks to the presence of the dogs. It is reminiscent of Stalin's

9-1 GCSE REVISION NOTES – ANIMAL FARM

use of the secret police to make sure he retained power.

Squealer continues to be a 'spin doctor', turning the animals against Snowball. Even Boxer adopts a new motto: 'Napoleon is always right' (41). Loyalty is extremely important to the horse, but initially he was 'vaguely troubled' by Napoleon's decision to end the debates.

Napoleon then performs a 'U' turn, deciding that the windmill should be built after all. Squealer has to explain that Napoleon only 'seemed to oppose the windmill' before, just so he could get get rid of Snowball, 'who was a dangerous character and a bad influence' (42). The animals accept the explanation, partly because 'the three dogs who happened to be with' Squealer, growl 'so threateningly' (43). This is another example of planned activity being underplayed by the narrator. If the narrator is to be considered omniscient, then the phrase 'happened to be' there is ironic.

Chapter Six

The deteriorating conditions that most of the animals have to suffer is emphasised by the description of them working 'like slaves' (44). They don't have any real freedom, anymore than they did under Mr Jones. The narrator uses the word 'voluntary' ironically, as the animals have to do extra work or suffer a reduction in rations: this is not an option many would choose (44).

Boxer's efforts are highlighted by the language used by the narrator. Images of him 'toiling up the slope inch by inch, his breath coming fast, the tips of his hoofs clawing at the ground and his great sides matted with sweat' make the reader wonder if his huge sacrifice is going to pay off or not (45).

Although the animals generally do a good job on the farm, 'unforeseen shortages' lead to Napoleon announcing that 'from now onwards Animal Farm' will 'engage in trade with neighboring farms' (46). The animals are assured that it won't be 'for any commercial purpose' (46). The trade will just be to obtain 'materials' which are 'urgently necessary' (47). How 'dog biscuits' can be on the list of

9-1 GCSE REVISION NOTES – ANIMAL FARM

necessities remains a moot point for the reader, if not for the animals, who accept Napoleon's viewpoint (46). However, there is a 'vague uneasiness' as some remember a resolution 'never to engage in trade' (47).

Squealer tells the animals it's 'pure imagination' to think such a resolution was passed (48). He puts it down to 'lies circulated by Snowball' (48). Once again, he is acting like a spin doctor to manipulate the animals.

We are introduced to a new character in the shape of Mr Whymper, who sounds weak judging by the name, which reminds us of an animal in pain. We are told the solicitor is a 'sly-looking man', so is not to be trusted (48). However, he is to be used as an 'intermediary between Animal Farm and the outside world' (47).

Like Stalin, who signed deals with Hitler and Churchill at different times during War War Two, Napoleon wavers between entering 'into a definite business agreement either with Mr Pilkington of Foxwood or with Mr Frederick of Pinchfield' (49). Additionally, like Stalin, the agreements are 'never' with 'both simultaneously' (49).

Meanwhile, the animals notice that the pigs have taken up residence in the farm house and are sleeping on beds. To clarify matters, the pigs' spokesman, Squealer, says: 'You did not suppose, surely, that there was ever a ruling against beds' (50). He makes the other animals feel foolish for thinking such a thing, especially as the relevant commandment has been altered to: 'No animal shall sleep in a bed with sheets' (50).

More bad news follows for the animals, as they wake up to discover that the windmill is 'in ruins' (51). Destruction has hit other parts of the farm too, as they see that 'an elm tree at the foot of the orchard' has 'been plucked up like a radish' (51). This simile suggests how small and insignificant Animal Farm is in the greater scheme of things, as a radish is a tiny vegetable. The fact that the 'flagstaff had blown down' indicates all the destruction was caused by a strong wind (51).

Napoleon, the opportunist that he is, uses the moment to increase the hatred felt towards Snowball. He puts the question in the other animals' heads first by asking: 'Do you know the enemy who has come in the night and overthrown our windmill?' (52). He then provides the answer: 'SNOWBALL!' (52). Instead of accepting the blame for a poorly constructed

9-1 GCSE REVISION NOTES – ANIMAL FARM

windmill, Napoleon has placed the blame elsewhere and increased his power over the other animals by suggesting that they are under threat from outside forces. Napoleon uses the moment to mobilise the animals into greater efforts, using slogans like: 'Long live Animal Farm!' (53).

Chapter Seven

Through the pathetic fallacy of the weather, the narrator reveals how harsh conditions are for the animals, who have to endure 'a hard frost' which does not break 'till well into February' (54).

We then hear that 'human beings' are pretending 'not to believe that it was Snowball who had destroyed the windmill' (54). The narrator uses the word 'pretended' ironically to convey the idea that the animals still do not trust human judgement despite all the evidence suggesting that they are right (54). Despite not trusting human judgement about the windmill 'walls being too thin', a decision is made to 'build the walls three feet thick this time' (54).

Propaganda seems to be more important than the actual conditions on Animal Farm to Napoloeon, which is often the case in totalitarian regimes. We discover: 'It was vitally necessary to conceal this fact [about starvation] from the outside world' (55). Of course, the reader may feel that Napoleon should concentrate on improving conditions rather than

9-1 GCSE REVISION NOTES – ANIMAL FARM

making 'use of Mr Whymper to spread a contrary impression' (55).

Nevertheless, 'something resembling a rebellion' begins with 'three Black Minorca pullets' smashing their eggs (56). The hens are upset when they discover they 'must surrender their eggs' to Napoleon, who 'had accepted, through Whymper, a contract for four hundred eggs a week' (56). However, the rebellion is quelled swifted, as the hens 'capitulated and went back to the lie nesting boxes' (56).

Napoleon tightens his grip on his populace, by using alarmist, scare tactics. The threat of Snowball looms larger and larger in the animals' collective imagination. The narrator reports that: 'Snowball was secretly frequenting the farm by night!' (57). The idea of him visiting under cover of the night makes him seem all the more dangerous.

Squealer announced that 'Snowball has sold himself to Frederick of Pinchfield Farm' (58). The animals then believe that Snowball is plotting an attack on Animal Farm.

The pigs, through Squealer, try to rewrite history by claiming that 'Snowball was in league with Jones from the very start!' (58). The pigs' spokesman tries to convince the other animals that Snowball tried to throw the Battle of the Cowshed, but even Boxer protests, saying: 'I do not believe that' (59).

Squealer goes on to describe 'the scene so graphically' that the animals begin to think they 'remember' The Battle of the Cowshed in the same way as the pigs would have them believe (60). For his opposition, Squealer casts 'a very ugly look at Boxer', which does not bode well for the horse (60).

Unsurprisingly at an assembly some days later, three of Napoleon's dogs attack Boxer, who is too strong for them. The big horse pins one down, but shows 'mercy' once Napoleon 'sharply' orders him 'to let the dog go' (61). This makes Boxer appear to be an even more sympathetic character, as he is never keen to take another's life.

The repression of opposition is common feature of totalitarian regimes. Napoleon's reaction to opponents is reminiscent of Stalin's purges in Russia. The animals are left disorientated by it all, not knowing 'which was more shocking - the treachery of the animals [...] or the cruel retribution' (62).

Ironically, the animals notice how beautiful Animal Farm is with 'the grass and the bursting

9-1 GCSE REVISION NOTES – ANIMAL FARM

hedges' being 'gilded by the level rays of the sun' (63). This idyllic scene contrasts with the awful bloodshed that the animals have just witnessed, making the description all the more poignant.

The animals have been stunned and shocked into silence by the pigs and the dogs, although 'these scenes of slaughter and terror were not what they looked forward to on that night when old Major first stirred them to rebellion (64). A lack of education prevents the animals from rebelling again, as although Clover realizes what has happened in 'her thoughts', she does not have 'the words to express them' (64). The narrator is implying that revolution is only possible with an educated underclass.

Clover takes to singing 'Beasts of England', but such is the level of repression at Animal Farm that even that has been 'abolished' (65). It is now 'forbidden to sing it' (65). Minimus's replacement song, does not 'come up to "Beasts of England"', but it is the official anthem nonetheless (65).

Chapter Eight

Doubts over the wording of the commandments continue, with Clover asking Muriel to read the sixth one aloud to her. It reads: 'No animal shall kill another without cause' (66). The last two words are italicized so the reader realizes that they have been added. Ironically, the narrator comments: 'Somehow or other the last two words had slipped out of the animals' memory' (66).

More cynicism follows as the narrator comments on Squealer reading 'lists of figures proving that the production of every foodstuff had increased' (67). The narrator comments in an understated way that 'there were days when they [the animals] felt that they would sooner have had less figures and more food' (67).

Napoleon's insistence on ceremony has led him to employ 'a black cockerel', who acts 'as a kind of trumpeter, letting out a loud "cock-a-doodle-doo" before' he spoke (67). Napoleon is forever tightening his grip on the community he governs. Furthermore, the other pigs have bestowed titles on him, such as: 'Father of All Animals, Terror of Mankind, Protector of the

9-1 GCSE REVISION NOTES – ANIMAL FARM

Sheepfold, Ducklings' Friend and the like' (67). Otherwise, he is always referred to reverentially now as 'our Leader' or 'Comrade Napoleon' (67). This is a true dictatorship in every sense of the word, with the masses expected to worship the leader.

To this aim, Napoleon employs his own poet, Minimus, to write flattering rhymes about him. Arguably, the most flattering line of his poem says that Comrade Napoleon is 'like the sun in the sky' (68). This suggests that Napoleon is a warm provider, meeting all animals' needs. However, the animals are virtually starving.

Meanwhile, Napoleon is deep in 'negotiations with Frederick and Pilkington' (69). The animals would 'greatly' prefer a deal with Pilkington, as Frederick is to be 'feared and hated' (69). They are so furious with Frederick for the reported 'cruelties' that he has inflicted on his animals that they want to 'attack Pinchfield Farm (70). Squealer advises them to 'avoid rash actions and trust in Comrade Napoleon's strategy' (70). This seemingly sensible advice ensures that Napoleon remains in full control of Animal Farm.

Nevertheless, it is Napoleon and his propaganda machine that has whipped the animals up into a state of frenzied hatred. Even his pigeons are ordered to change their slogan from 'Death to Humanity' to 'Death to Frederick' (70).

His ego knows no bounds, as even the new windmill is named 'Napoleon Mill' (71). Although the animals deserve most of the credit of overcoming 'every difficulty', it is Napoleon who will get the ultimate credit by naming the building after himself (71).

Soon afterwards, the animals are 'struck dumb' by Napoleon's announcement that 'he had sold the pile of timber to Frederick' (72). This is quickly explained as the animals are told that Snowball had 'never' been to Pinchfield Farm; instead, he 'had in reality been a pensioner of Pilkington for years past' (72). The uneducated animals are all too ready to accept this new version of events.

However, the bank notes used for payment turn out to be 'forgeries' (73). Napoleon pronounces 'the death sentence upon Frederick' and tells the animals to expect an attach (73).

At least, Napoleon predicts the future with some accuracy, as Frederick and his followers attack 'the very next morning' (73). Smacking of over-confidence, Napoleon then predicts that the humans cannot 'knock it [the windmill] down in a week' (74). This time, he is wrong as after the

9-1 GCSE REVISION NOTES – ANIMAL FARM

humans use 'blasting powder' on it, 'the windmill' ceases 'to exist' (74, 75).

The writer uses personification to emphasize how angry the animals are at the windmill's destruction. We discover that 'the fear and despair' are 'drowned in the rage against this vile, contemptible act' (75). The language make it seem like 'rage' has swept over them like a huge wave.

Eventually, the animals are victorious, but that's not due to Squealer, 'who had unaccountably been absent during the fighting' (76). Nevertheless, the pig wants to share in getting some credit, calling the battle 'our victory' (76).

Using symbols and ceremony, the regime reasserts its authority over the animals. They begin to believe it was indeed 'a great victory', when they see 'the green flag flying', and hear 'the gun firing again' and 'the speech that Napoleon made' (77).

Shortly afterwards, the animals are dismayed to hear that Napoleon is 'dying' (78). Of course, he is just suffering from a hangover, as his 'solemn decree' outlawing the 'drinking of alcohol' suggests (78). This commandment is altered by Squealer, who is caught with a 'broken' ladder, 'a lantern, a paintbrush and an overturned pot of paint' (79). Next time the animals read it, they notice the Commandment reads: 'No animal shall drink alcohol to excess' (79). Ironically, the animals think they have 'remembered' it 'wrong' (79). Once again, their lack of education allows them to be manipulated easily.

9-1 GCSE REVISION NOTES – ANIMAL FARM

Chapter Nine

We discover that 'when the laws of Animal Farm were first formulated, the retiring age had been fixed for horses and pigs at twelve' (80). With Boxer soon to reach that age, we wonder if he will be allowed to retire. The animals probably believe it will happen, as they even believe they have 'more straw in the stalls' and suffer 'less from fleas' than they did under Jones (81). That notion is partly aided by Squealer's language that keeps the animals from revolting. Squealer never refers to a 'reduction' of rations, preferring to use 'readjustment' instead; this euphemism sounds less harsh to the starving animals.

The inequality becomes even more glaringly obvious when a new rule is introduced, stating that 'when a pig and any other animal' meet 'on the path, the other animal must stand aside' (82).

Nevertheless, the animals perceive that they have 'greater dignity' than they had before (83). Instead of food and equality, they have to settle for 'more songs, more speeches, more processions' (83). Ironically, Napoleon introduces 'a Spontaneous Demonstration' once a week, which by its planned nature is anything but spontaneous (83). However, these activities do keep the animals busy, giving them less time to think of their 'empty' bellies (84).

Moses the raven is allowed to return to Animal Farm, and is given 'an allowance of a gill of beer a day' (85). Clearly, he is now an instrument of the totalitarian regime. By allowing Moses to preach about SugarCandy Mountain, the pigs are effectively taking the animals' minds off the harsh present: instead they are thinking of a beautiful life after death. In this state, the animals are less likely to revolt.

Soon after this revelation, we discover that 'Boxer has fallen' (86). The big horse has 'glazed' eyes and with 'a thin stream of blood' trickling from 'his mouth', he appears to be near death (86). Although Napoleon says he's arranged for Boxer 'to be treated in the hospital at Willingdon', the animals feel 'a little uneasy at this' (87). Rather than distrusting their shifty leader, they do 'not like to think of their sick comrade in the hands of human beings' (87).

When Boxer is driven off by 'a sly-looking man in a low-crowned bowler hat', the signs are unpromising (88). Benjamin is first to realize that Boxer is being taken 'to the knacker's' (88). It is the most dramatic moment in the novel, with

9-1 GCSE REVISION NOTES – ANIMAL FARM

Benjamin reading aloud, 'galloping' and 'braying at the top of his voice' (88). It is completely uncharacteristic of him to act in this way, so it makes the whole scene more shocking.

Boxer attempts to escape and initially the animals see his face appearing 'at the small window at the back of the van' (89). When his face disappears, the narrative relies on sound imagery to convey what is happening. The animals hear 'the sound of a tremendous drumming of hoofs inside the van' (90). This sound grows 'fainter' and dies away, like Boxer's life (90). The sound imagery adds effectively to the drama, with the fading sounds resonating with the reader.

As usual, Squealer does his best to cover up the truth. This time the pig explains that 'the van had previously been the property of the knacker, and had been bought by the veterinary surgeon, who had not yet painted the old name out' (90). It seems feasible enough, but even if the animals believe it, the readers won't.

The pigs' corruption appears to be boundless as they plan a 'memorial banquet in Boxer's honour' (91). That sounds the moral thing to do on the face of it, but the delivery of 'a wooden crate' suggests that the pigs are planning a drunken party (91). The narrator says the pigs 'acquired the money to buy themselves another case of whisky' from 'somewhere or other', which tells the reader that they've used the proceeds from the sale of Boxer to the knacker's for this purpose (91).

Chapter Ten

We are told in the briefest terms that some time has elapsed: 'Years passed'. The short sentence adds tension to the narrative. It feels even more matter-of-fact than earlier.

We discover that Clover still hasn't retired, despite being 'two years past the retiring age', and that Benjamin is 'more morose and taciturn than ever' (92). Meanwhile, Napoleon and Squealer are fatter than ever, suggesting that they've been enjoying the good life while the rest of the animals have been struggling.

Indeed, 'the luxuries of which Snowball had once taught the animals to dream' are 'no longer talked about' (93). Napoleon denounces such ideas, saying they run 'contrary to the spirit of Animalism' (93). He encourages 'working hard and living frugally', but his 'twenty-four stone' frame implies that he doesn't practise what he preaches (93, 92). In other words, he's a hypocrit.

Meanwhile, Squealer is still bamboozling the animals with 'lists of figures', which prove 'that everything' is 'getting better and better' (94). The spin doctor is excellent at manipulating the ignorant animals.

Despite the awful conditions, the animals 'hearts' swell 'with imperishable pride' when they hear 'the gun booming', and see 'the green flag fluttering' (95). Through simple ceremonies and traditions, the pigs still exercise control over the other animals' minds.

However, the animals are shocked again when they see Squealer 'walking on his hind legs' (96). Later, it gets worse, when they see 'Napoleon himself, majestically upright', carrying 'a whip in his trotter' (96). The symbol of the whip indicates that the other animals are enslaved, no matter what they think.

The sheep have been taught to sing a new song: 'Four legs good, two legs better' (97). All opposition has been drowned out.

Now the seven commandments have been reduced to just one: 'ALL ANIMALS ARE EQUAL BUT SOME ARE MORE EQUAL THAN OTHERS' (97). Obviously, the words 'more equal' are meaningless, but the confusion they cause means the pigs can get away with having an elevated status.

9-1 GCSE REVISION NOTES – ANIMAL FARM

The other animals carry on as normal, working 'diligently, hardly raising their faces from the ground' (98). The reader may have a great deal of sympathy for these honest but ignorant creatures, who never receive the fruits of their labours. They are simply exploited by the pigs, who are entertaining human farmers that evening in the farmhouse.

Mr Pilkington makes a speech, extolling the virtues of Animal Farm, highlighting 'the most up-to-date methods', 'discipline' and 'orderliness' (99). It is clear that he has great admiration for Napoleon and his farm. In particular, Pilkington admires the fact that 'the lower animals on Animal Farm' do 'more work and' receive 'less food than any other animals in the country' (100). He likens the lower animals to 'lower classes' of human being (100). He is so unpalatable as a character that the narrator's socialist political message is conveyed subtly and effectively.

On the surface, Animal Farm is run on socialist lines, as Napoleon claims the 'title-deeds' are 'owned by the pigs jointly' (101). Nevertheless, he wields absolute power, as we have seen throughout the narrative.

Lastly, we discover that Napoleon had changed the name of the farm back to 'The Manor Farm'

(102). He is just as untrustworthy as any human being, which is why when the other animals look 'from pig to man, and from man to pig, and pig to man again' it is impossible to tell the difference (102). This memorable image of pig merging into man and vice versa sticks in the reader's mind, making the ending of this dystopian piece of fiction extremely bleak.

9-1 GCSE REVISION NOTES – ANIMAL FARM

Essay writing tips

<u>Use a variety of connectives</u>

Have a look of this list of connectives. Which of these would you choose to use?

'ADDING' DISCOURSE MARKERS

- AND
- ALSO
- AS WELL AS
- MOREOVER
- TOO
- FURTHERMORE
- ADDITIONALLY

I hope you chose 'additionally', 'furthermore' and 'moreover'. Don't be afraid to use the lesser discourse markers, as they are also useful. Just avoid using those ones over and over again. I've seen essays from Key Stage 4 students that use the same discourse marker for the opening sentence of each paragraph! Needless to say, those essays didn't get great marks!

Okay, here are some more connectives for you to look at. Select the best ones.

'SEQUENCING' DISCOURSE MARKERS

- NEXT
- FIRSTLY
- SECONDLY
- THIRDLY
- FINALLY
- MEANWHILE
- AFTER
- THEN
- SUBSEQUENTLY

This time, I hope you chose 'subsequently' and 'meanwhile'.

Here are some more connectives for you to 'grade'!

'ILLUSTRATING / EXEMPLIFYING' DISCOURSE MARKERS

- FOR EXAMPLE
- SUCH AS
- FOR INSTANCE
- IN THE CASE OF

9-1 GCSE REVISION NOTES – ANIMAL FARM

- AS REVEALED BY
- ILLUSTRATED BY

I'd probably go for 'illustrated by' or even 'as exemplified by' (which is not in the list!). Please feel free to add your own examples to the lists. Strong connectives impress examiners. Don't forget it! That's why I want you to look at some more.

'CAUSE & EFFECT' DISCOURSE MARKERS

- BECAUSE
- SO
- THEREFORE
- THUS
- CONSEQUENTLY
- HENCE

I'm going for 'consequently' this time. How about you? What about the next batch?

'COMPARING' DISCOURSE MARKERS

- SIMILARLY
- LIKEWISE
- AS WITH
- LIKE

- EQUALLY
- IN THE SAME WAY

I'd choose 'similarly' this time. Still some more to go.

'QUALIFYING' DISCOURSE MARKERS

- BUT
- HOWEVER
- WHILE
- ALTHOUGH
- UNLESS
- EXCEPT
- APART FROM
- AS LONG AS

It's 'however' for me!

'CONTRASTING' DISCOURSE MARKERS

- WHEREAS
- INSTEAD OF
- ALTERNATIVELY
- OTHERWISE
- UNLIKE

9-1 GCSE REVISION NOTES – ANIMAL FARM

- ON THE OTHER HAND
- CONVERSELY

I'll take 'conversely' or 'alternatively' this time.

'EMPHASISING' DISCOURSE MARKERS

- ABOVE ALL
- IN PARTICULAR
- ESPECIALLY
- SIGNIFICANTLY
- INDEED
- NOTABLY

You can breathe a sigh of relief now! It's over! No more connectives. However, now I want to put our new found skills to use in our essays.

Useful information/Glossary

Allegory: extended metaphor, like the grim reaper representing death, e.g. Scrooge symbolizing capitalism.

Alliteration: same consonant sound repeating, e.g. 'She sells sea shells'.

Allusion: reference to another text/person/place/event.

Ascending tricolon: sentence with three parts, each increasing in power, e.g. 'ringing, drumming, shouting'.

Aside: character speaking so some characters cannot hear what is being said. Sometimes, an aside is directly to the audience. It's a dramatic technique which reveals the character's inner thoughts and feelings.

Assonance: same vowel sounds repeating, e.g. 'Oh no, won't Joe go?'

Bathos: abrupt change from sublime to ridiculous for humorous effect.

Blank verse: lines of unrhymed iambic pentameter.

Compressed time: when the narrative is fast-forwarding through the action.

Descending tricolon: sentence with three parts, each decreasing in power, e.g. 'shouting, talking, whispering'.

Denouement: tying up loose ends, the resolution.

Diction: choice of words or vocabulary.

Didactic: used to describe literature designed to inform, instruct or pass on a moral message.

Dilated time: opposite compressed time, here the narrative is in slow motion.

Direct address: second person narrative, predominantly using the personal pronoun 'you'.

Dramatic action verb: manifests itself in physical action, e.g. I punched him in the face.

Dramatic irony: audience knows something that the character is unaware of.

Ellipsis: leaving out part of the story and allowing the reader to fill in the narrative gap.

End-stopped lines: poetic lines that end with punctuation.

9-1 GCSE REVISION NOTES – ANIMAL FARM

Epistolary: letter or correspondence-driven narrative.

Flashback/Analepsis: going back in time to the past, interrupting the chronological sequence.

Flashforward/Prolepsis: going forward in time to the future, interrupting the chronological sequence.

Foreshadowing/Adumbrating: suggestion of plot developments that will occur later in the narrative.

Gothic: another strand of Romanticism, typically with a wild setting, a sensitive heroine, an older man with a 'piercing gaze', discontinuous structure, doppelgangers, guilt and the 'unspeakable' (according to Eve Kosofsky Sedgwick).

Hamartia: character flaw, leading to that character's downfall.

Hyperbole: exaggeration for effect.

Iambic pentameter: a line of ten syllables beginning with a lighter stress alternating with a heavier stress in its perfect form, which sounds like a heartbeat. The stress falls on the even syllables, numbers: 2, 4, 6, 8 and 10, e.g. 'When now I think you can behold such sights'.

Intertextuality: links to other literary texts.

Irony: amusing or cruel reversal of expected outcome or words meaning the opposite to their literal meaning.

Metafiction/Romantic irony: self-conscious exposure of the devices used to create 'the truth' within a work of fiction.

Motif: recurring image use of language or idea that connects the narrative together and creates a theme or mood, e.g. 'green light' in *The Great Gatsby*.

Oxymoron: contradictory terms combined, e.g. deafening silence.

Pastiche: imitation of another's work.

Pathetic fallacy: a form of personification whereby inanimate objects show human attributes, e.g. 'the sea smiled benignly'. The originator of the term, John Ruskin in 1856, used 'the cruel, crawling foam', from Kingsley's *The Sands of Dee*, as an example to clarify what he meant by the 'morbid' nature of pathetic fallacy.

Personification: concrete or abstract object made human, often simply achieved by using a capital letter or a personal pronoun, e.g. 'Nature', or describing a ship as 'she'.

Pun/Double entendre: a word with a double meaning, usually employed in witty wordplay but not always.

Retrospective: account of events after they have occurred.

Romanticism: genre celebrating the power of imagination, spriritualism and nature.

Semantic/lexical field: related words about a single concept, e.g. king, queen and prince are all concerned with royalty.

Soliloquy: character thinks aloud, but is not heard by other characters (unlike in a monologue) giving the audience access to inner thoughts and feelings.

Style: choice of language, form and structure, and effects produced.

Synecdoche: one part of something referring to the whole, e.g. Carker's teeth represent him in *Dombey and Son*.

9-1 GCSE REVISION NOTES – ANIMAL FARM

Syntax: the way words and sentences are placed together.

Tetracolon climax: sentence with four parts, culminating with the last part, e.g. 'I have nothing to offer but blood, toil, tears, and sweat ' (Winston Churchill).

ABOUT THE AUTHOR

Joe Broadfoot is a secondary school teacher of English and a soccer journalist, who also writes fiction and literary criticism. His former experiences as a DJ took him to far-flung places such as Tokyo, Kobe, Beijing, Hong Kong, Jakarta, Cairo, Dubai, Cannes, Oslo, Bergen and Bodo. He is now PGCE and CELTA-qualified with QTS, a first-class honours degree in Literature and an MA in Victorian Studies (majoring in Charles Dickens). Drama is close to his heart as he acted in 'Macbeth' and 'A Midsummer Night's Dream' at the Royal Northern College of Music in Manchester. More recently, he has been teaching 'A' Level and GCSE English Literature and IGCSE and GCSE English Language to students at secondary schools in Buckinghamshire, Kent and in south and west London.